STAR BRIGHT
QUILTS

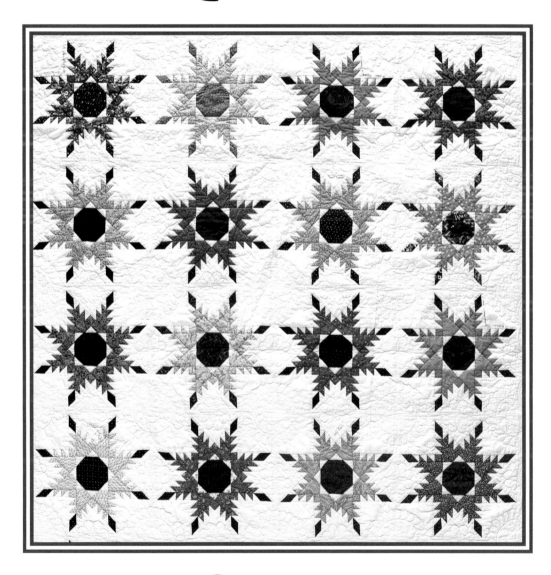

Oxmoor House ®

STAR BRIGHT QUILTS

©1995 by Oxmoor House, Inc.

Book Division of Southern Progress Corporation
P.O. Box 2463, Birmingham, AL 35201

Published by Oxmoor House, Inc., and
Leisure Arts, Inc.

Library of Congress Catalog Number: 94-69240
ISBN: 0-8487-1264-1

Manufactured in the United States of America
First Printing 1995

Editor-in-Chief: Nancy J. Fitzpatrick
Editorial Director, Special Interest Publications:
  Ann H. Harvey
Senior Crafts Editor: Susan Ramey Cleveland
Senior Editor, Editorial Services: Olivia Kindig Wells
Art Director: James Boone

STAR BRIGHT QUILTS

Editor: Patricia Wilens
Editorial Assistant: Janica Lynn York
Copy Editor: Jennifer K. Mathews
Senior Designer: Larry Hunter
Designer: Carol Loria
Illustrator: Kelly Davis
Publishing Systems Administrator: Rick Tucker
Senior Photographer: John O'Hagan
Photo Stylist: Katie Stoddard
Production and Distribution Director: Phillip Lee
Production Manager: Gail H. Morris
Associate Production Manager: Theresa L. Beste
Production Assistant: Marianne Jordan

Contents

Dear Quilting Friends:

Star light, star bright, first star I see tonight—I wish I may, I wish I might have the wish I wish tonight.

Remember that childhood litany? Stars have always been symbols of our wishes (wish upon a star), hopes (reach for a star), and aspirations (hitch your wagon to a star). A star led the Magi to the miracle in Bethlehem. A star was the signpost by which Wendy, Michael, and John found Neverland. Stars top Christmas trees and magic wands, and adorn the heavens with a light show unsurpassed by lasers or rocket launches. Is it any wonder that our quilting foremothers chose stars as themes for so many of our traditional quilt patterns?

In this book, we give you 12 sparkling quilt designs. If you're a beginner or just looking for a simple-to-make quilt, check out the starkly beautiful *In the Bleak Midwinter* on page 32 or the bold blue-and-white *Storm at Sea* on page 46. If you're looking for a challenge, try *Golden Double Wedding Ring* on page 12 or *Feathered Friends* on page 20. Whatever your skill level or quilting aspirations, you're sure to find just the right project to make you the star of your quilting circle.

Perhaps a line borrowed from Jiminy Cricket says it best: when you wish upon a star, your quilts come true.

Happy Stitching,

Susan Ramey Cleveland

WORKSHOP

Selecting Fabrics

The best fabric for quilts is 100% cotton. Yardage requirements are based on 44"-wide fabric and allow for shrinkage. All fabrics, including backing, should be machine-washed, dried, and pressed before cutting. Use warm water and detergent but not fabric softener.

Necessary Notions

- Scissors
- Rotary cutter and mat
- Acrylic rulers
- Template plastic
- Pencils for marking cutting lines
- Sewing needles
- Sewing thread
- Sewing machine
- Seam ripper
- Pins
- Iron and ironing board
- Quilting needles
- Thimble
- Hand quilting thread
- Machine quilting thread

Making Templates

A template is a duplication of a printed pattern, made from a sturdy material, which is traced onto fabric. Many regular shapes such as squares and triangles can be marked directly on the fabric with a ruler, but you need templates for other shapes. Some quiltmakers use templates for all shapes.

You can trace patterns directly onto template plastic. Or make a template by tracing a pattern onto graph paper and gluing the paper to posterboard or sandpaper. (Sandpaper will not slip on fabric.)

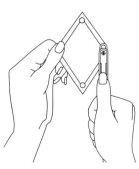

When a large pattern is given in two pieces, make one template for the complete piece.

Cut out the template on the marked line. It is important that a template be traced, marked, and cut accurately. If desired, punch out corner dots with a ⅛"-diameter hole punch (**Diagram 1**).

Diagram 1

Mark each template with its letter and grain line. Verify the template's accuracy, placing it over the printed pattern. Any discrepancy, however small, is multiplied many times as the quilt is assembled. Another way to check templates' accuracy is to make a test block before cutting more pieces.

Tracing Templates on Fabric

For hand piecing, templates should be cut to the finished size of the piece so seam lines can be marked on the fabric. Avoiding the selvage, place the template *facedown* on the *wrong* side of the fabric, aligning the template grain line with the straight grain. Hold the template firmly and trace around it. Repeat as needed, leaving ½" between tracings (**Diagram 2**).

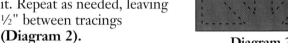

Diagram 2

For machine piecing, templates should include seam allowances. These templates are used in the same manner as for hand piecing, but you can mark the fabric using common lines for efficient cutting (**Diagram 3**). Mark corners on fabric through holes in the template.

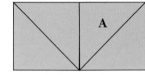

Diagram 3

For hand or machine piecing, use window templates to enhance accuracy by drawing and cutting out both cutting and sewing lines. The guidance of a drawn seam line is very useful for sewing set-in seams, when pivoting at a precise point is critical. Used on the right side of the fabric, window templates help you cut specific motifs with accuracy (**Diagram 4**).

Diagram 4

For hand appliqué, templates should be made the finished size. Place templates *faceup* on the *right* side of the fabric. Position tracings at least ½" apart (**Diagram 5**). Add a ¼" seam allowance around pieces when cutting.

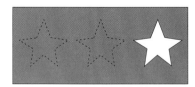

Diagram 5

Cutting

Grain Lines

Woven threads form the fabric's grain. Lengthwise grain, parallel to the selvages, has the least stretch; crosswise grain has a little more give.

Long strips such as borders should be cut lengthwise whenever possible and cut first to ensure that you have the necessary length. Usually, other pieces can be cut aligned with either grain.

Bias is the 45° diagonal line between the two grain directions. Bias has the most stretch and is used for curving strips such as flower stems. Bias is often preferred for binding.

Never use the selvage (finished edge). Selvage does not react to washing, drying, and pressing like the rest of the fabric and may pucker when the finished quilt is laundered.

Rotary Cutting

A rotary cutter, used with a protective mat and a ruler, takes getting used to but is very efficient for cutting strips, squares, and triangles. A rotary cutter is fast because you can measure and cut multiple layers with a single stroke, without templates or marking. It is also more accurate than cutting with scissors because fabrics remain flat and do not move during cutting.

Because the blade is very sharp, be sure to get a rotary cutter with a safety guard. Keep the guard in the safe position at all times, except when making a cut. *Always keep the cutter out of the reach of children.*

Use the cutter with a self-healing mat. A good mat for cutting strips is at least 23" wide.

1. Squaring the fabric is the first step in accurate cutting. Fold the fabric with selvages aligned. With the yardage to your right, align a small square ruler with the fold near the cut edge. Place a long ruler against the left side of the square **(Diagram 6)**. Keeping the long ruler in place, remove the square. Hold the ruler in place with your left hand as you cut, rolling the cutter *away from you* along the ruler's edge with a steady motion. You can move your left hand along the ruler as you cut, but do not change the position of the ruler. *Keep your fingers away from the ruler's edge when cutting.*

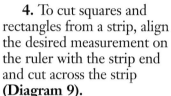

Diagram 6

2. Open the fabric. If the cut was not accurately perpendicular to the fold, the edge will be V-shaped instead of straight **(Diagram 7)**. Correct the cut if necessary.

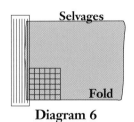

Correct cut · Not cut at 90° angle

Fold

Diagram 7

3. With a transparent ruler, you can measure and cut at the same time. Fold the fabric in half again, aligning the selvages with the fold, making four layers that line up perfectly along the cut edge. Project instructions designate the strip width needed. Position the ruler to measure the correct distance from the edge **(Diagram 8)** and cut. The blade will easily cut through all four layers. Check the strip to be sure the cut is straight. The strip length is the width of the fabric, approximately 43" to 44". Using the ruler again, trim selvages, cutting about ⅜" from each end.

Diagram 8

4. To cut squares and rectangles from a strip, align the desired measurement on the ruler with the strip end and cut across the strip **(Diagram 9)**.

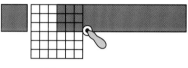

Diagram 9

5. Cut triangles from squares or rectangles. Cutting instructions often direct you to cut a square in half or in quarters diagonally to make right triangles, and this technique can apply to rectangles, too **(Diagram 10)**. The outside edges of the square or rectangle are on the straight of the grain, so triangle sides cut on the diagonal are bias.

6. Some projects in this book use a time-saving technique called strip piecing. With this method, strips are joined to make a pieced band. Cut across the seams of this band to cut preassembled units **(Diagram 11)**.

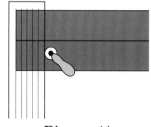

Diagram 11

Machine Piecing

Your sewing machine does not have to be a new, computerized model. A good straight stitch is all that's necessary, but it may be helpful to have a nice satin stitch for appliqué. Clean and oil your machine regularly, use good-quality thread, and replace needles frequently.

1. Patches for machine piecing are cut with the seam allowance included, but the sewing line is not usually marked. Therefore, a way to make a consistent ¼" seam is essential. Some presser feet have a right toe that is ¼" from the needle. Other machines have an adjustable needle that can be set for a ¼" seam. If your machine has neither feature, experiment to find how the fabric must be placed to make a ¼" seam. Mark this position on the presser foot or throat plate.

2. Use a stitch length that makes a strong seam but is not too difficult to remove with a seam ripper. The best setting is usually 10 to 12 stitches per inch.

3. Pin only when really necessary. If a straight seam is less than 4" and does not have to match an adjoining seam, pinning is not necessary.

4. When intersecting seams must align **(Diagram 12)**, match the units with right sides facing and push a pin through both seams at the seam line. Turn the pinned unit to the right side to check the alignment; then pin securely. As you sew, remove each pin just before the needle reaches it.

Figure 1   Figure 2

Intersecting seams aligned   Intersecting seams not aligned

Diagram 12

5. Block assembly diagrams are used throughout this book to show how pieces should be joined. Make small units first; then join them in rows and continue joining rows to finish the block **(Diagram 13)**. Blocks are joined in the same manner to complete the quilt top.

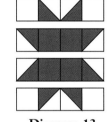

Diagram 13

6. Chain piecing saves time. Stack pieces to be sewn in pairs, with right sides facing. Join the first pair as usual. At the end of the seam, do not backstitch, cut the thread, or lift the presser foot. Just feed in the next pair of pieces—the machine will make a few stitches between pieces before the needle strikes the second piece of fabric. Continue sewing in this way until all pairs are joined. Stack the chain of pieces until you are ready to clip them apart **(Diagram 14)**.

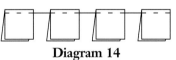

Diagram 14

7. Most seams are sewn straight across, from raw edge to raw edge. Since they will be crossed by other

seams, they do not require backstitching to secure them.

8. When piecing diamonds or other angled seams, you may need to make set-in seams. For these, always mark the corner dots (shown on the patterns) on the fabric pieces. Stitch one side, starting at the outside edge and being careful not to sew beyond the dot into the seam allowance **(Diagram 15, Figure A)**. Backstitch. Align the other side of the piece as needed, with right sides facing. Sew from the dot to the outside edge **(Figure B)**.

9. Sewing curved seams requires extra care. First, mark the centers of both the convex (outward) and concave (inward) curves **(Diagram 16)**. Staystitch just inside the seam allowance of both pieces. Clip the concave piece to the stitching **(Figure A)**. With right sides facing and raw edges aligned, pin the two patches together at the center **(Figure B)** and at the left edge **(Figure C)**. Sew from edge to center, stopping frequently to check that the raw edges are aligned. Stop at the center with the needle down. Raise the presser foot and pin the pieces together from the center to the right edge. Lower the foot and continue to sew. Press seam allowances toward the concave curve **(Figure D)**.

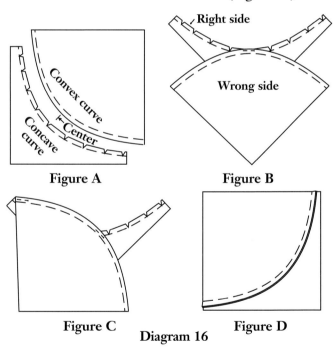

Right side

Convex curve

Concave curve

Center

Wrong side

Figure A   **Figure B**

Figure C   **Diagram 16**   **Figure D**

Hand Piecing

Make a running stitch of 8 to 10 stitches per inch along the marked seam line on the wrong side of the fabric. Don't pull the fabric as you sew; let the pieces lie relaxed in your hand. Sew from seam line to seam line, not from edge to edge as in machine piecing.

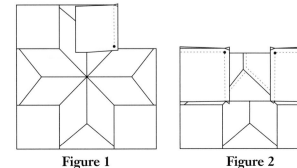

Figure 1   **Figure 2**

Diagram 15

When ending a line of stitching, backstitch over the last stitch and make a loop knot **(Diagram 17).**

Match seams and points accurately, pinning patches together before piecing. Align match points as described in Step 4 under Machine Piecing.

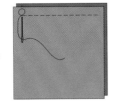

Diagram 17

When joining units where several seams meet, do not sew over seam allowances; sew *through* them at the match point **(Diagram 18).** When four or more seams meet, press the seam allowances in the same direction to reduce bulk **(Diagram 19).**

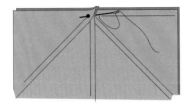

Diagram 18

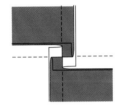

Diagram 19

Pressing

Careful pressing is necessary for precise piecing. Press each seam as you go. Sliding the iron back and forth may push the seam out of shape. Use an up-and-down motion, lifting the iron from spot to spot. Press the seam flat on the wrong side. Open the piece and, on the right side, press both seam allowances to one side (usually toward the darker fabric). Pressing the seam open leaves tiny gaps through which batting may beard.

Appliqué

Traditional Hand Appliqué

Hand appliqué requires that you turn under a seam allowance around the shape to prevent frayed edges.

1. Trace around the template on the right side of the fabric. This line indicates where to turn the seam allowance. Cut each piece approximately ¼" outside the line.

2. For simple shapes, turn the edges by pressing the seam allowance to the back; complex shapes may require basting the seam allowance. Sharp points and strong curves are best appliquéd with freezer paper. Clip curves to make a smooth edge. With practice, you can work without pressing seam allowances, turning edges under with the needle as you sew.

3. Do not turn under any seam allowance that will be covered by another appliqué piece.

4. To stitch, use one strand of cotton-wrapped polyester sewing thread in a color that matches the appliqué. Use a slipstitch, but keep the stitch very small on the surface. Working from right to left (or left to right if you're left-handed), pull the needle through the

base fabric and catch only a few threads on the folded edge of the appliqué. Reinsert the needle into the base fabric, under the top thread on the appliqué edge to keep the thread from tangling **(Diagram 20).**

5. An alternative to slipstitching is to work a decorative buttonhole stitch around each figure **(Diagram 21).**

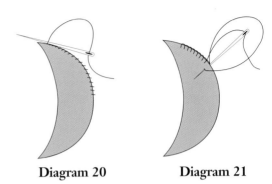

Diagram 20   **Diagram 21**

Freezer Paper Hand Appliqué

Supermarket freezer paper saves time because it eliminates the need for basting seam allowances.

1. Trace the template onto the *dull* side of the freezer paper and cut the paper on the marked line. *Note:* If a design is not symmetrical, turn the template over and trace a mirror image so the fabric piece won't be reversed when you cut it out.

2. Pin the freezer-paper shape, with its *shiny side* up, to the *wrong side* of the fabric. Following the paper shape and adding a scant ¼" seam allowance, cut out the fabric piece. Do not remove pins.

3. Using just the tip of a dry iron, press the seam allowance to the shiny side of the paper. Be careful not to touch the freezer paper with the iron.

4. Appliqué the piece to the background as in traditional appliqué. Trim the fabric from behind the shape, leaving ¼" seam allowances. Separate the freezer paper from the fabric with your fingernail and pull gently to remove it. If you prefer not to trim the background fabric, pull out the freezer paper before you complete stitching.

5. Sharp points require special attention. Turn the point down and press it **(Diagram 22, Figure A).** Fold the seam allowance on one side over the point and press **(Figure B)**; then fold the other seam allowance over the point and press **(Figure C).**

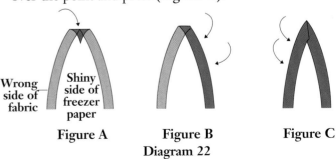

Wrong side of fabric   Shiny side of freezer paper

Figure A   **Figure B**   **Figure C**

Diagram 22

6. When pressing curved edges, clip sharp inward curves **(Diagram 23).** If the shape doesn't curve smoothly, separate the paper from the fabric with your fingernail and try again.

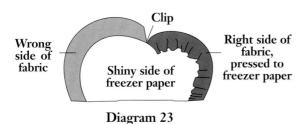

Diagram 23

7. Remove the pins when all seam allowances have been pressed to the freezer paper. Position the prepared appliqué right side up on the background fabric. Press to adhere it to the background fabric.

Machine Appliqué

A machine-sewn satin stitch makes a neat edging. For machine appliqué, cut appliqué pieces without adding seam allowances.

Using fusible web to adhere pieces to the background adds a stiff extra layer to the appliqué and is not appropriate for some quilts. It is best used on small pieces, difficult fabrics, or for wall hangings and accessories in which added stiffness is acceptable. The web prevents fraying and shifting during appliqué.

Place tear-away stabilizer under the background fabric behind the appliqué. Machine-stitch the appliqué edges with a satin stitch or close-spaced zigzag **(Diagram 24).** Test the stitch length and width on a sample first. Use an open-toed presser foot. Remove the stabilizer when appliqué is complete.

Diagram 24

Measuring Borders

Because seams may vary and fabrics may stretch a bit, opposite sides of your assembled quilt top may not be the same measurement. You can (and should) correct this when you add borders.

Measure the length of each side of the quilt. Trim the side border strips to match the *shorter* of the two sides. Join borders to the quilt as described below, easing the longer side of the quilt to fit the border. Join borders to the top and bottom edges in the same manner.

Straight Borders

Side borders are usually added first **(Diagram 25).** With right sides facing and raw edges aligned, pin the center of one border strip to the center of one side of

Diagram 25

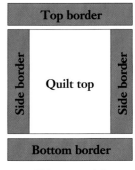

Diagram 26

the quilt top. Pin the border to the quilt at each end and then pin along the side as desired. Machine-stitch with the border strip on top. Press the seam allowance toward the border. Trim excess border fabric at each end. In the same manner, add the border to the opposite side and then the top and bottom borders **(Diagram 26).**

Mitered Borders

1. Measure your quilt sides. Trim the side border strips to fit the shorter side *plus* the width of the border *plus* 2".

2. Center the measurement of the shorter side on one border strip, placing a pin at each end and at the center of the measurement.

3. With right sides facing and raw edges aligned, match the pins on the border strip to the center and corners of the longer side of the quilt. (Border fabric will extend beyond the corners.)

4. Start machine-stitching at the top pin, backstitching to lock the stitches. Continue to sew, easing the quilt between pins. Stop at the last pin and backstitch. Join remaining borders in the same manner. Press seam allowances toward borders.

5. With right sides facing, fold the quilt diagonally, aligning the raw edges of adjacent borders. Pin securely **(Diagram 27).**

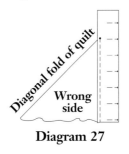

Diagram 27

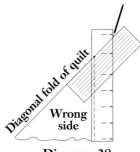

Diagram 28

6. Align a yardstick or quilter's ruler along the diagonal fold **(Diagram 28).** Holding the ruler firmly, mark a line from the end of the border seam to the raw edge.

7. Start machine-stitching at the beginning of the marked line, backstitch, and then stitch on the line out to the raw edge.

8. Unfold the quilt to be sure that the corner lies flat. Correct the stitching if necessary. Trim the seam allowance to ¼".

9. Miter the remaining corners in the same manner. Press the corner seams open.

Quilting Without Marking

Some quilts can be quilted in-the-ditch (right along the seam line), outline-quilted (¼" from the seam line), or echo-quilted (lines of quilting rippling outward from the design like waves on a pond). These methods can be used without any marking at all. If you are machine quilting, simply use the edge of your presser foot and the seam line as a guide. If you are hand quilting, by the time you have pieced a quilt top, your eye will be practiced enough for you to produce straight, even quilting without the guidance of marked lines.

Marking Quilting Designs

Many quilters like to mark the entire top at one time, a practice that requires long-lasting markings. The most common tool for this purpose is a sharp **pencil.** However, most pencils are made with an oil-based graphite lead, which often will not wash out completely. Look for a high-quality artist's pencil marked "2H" or higher (the higher the number, the harder the lead, and the lighter the line it will make). Sharpen the pencil frequently to keep the line on the fabric thin and light. Or try a mechanical pencil with a 0.5-mm lead. It will maintain a fine line without sharpening.

While you are in the art supply store, get a **white plastic eraser** (brand name Magic Rub). This eraser, used by professional drafters and artists, will cleanly remove the carbon smudges left by pencil lead without fraying the fabric or leaving eraser crumbs.

Water- and **air-soluble marking pens** are convenient, but controversial, marking tools. Some quilters have found that the marks reappear, often up to several years later, while others have no problems with them.

Be sure to test these pens on each fabric you plan to mark and *follow package directions exactly.* Because the inks can be permanently set by heat, be very careful with a marked quilt. Do not leave it in your car on a hot day and never touch it with an iron until the marks have been removed. Plan to complete the quilting within a year after marking it with a water-soluble pen.

Air-soluble pens are best for marking small sections at a time. The marks disappear within 24 to 48 hours, but the ink remains in the fabric until it is washed. After the quilt is completed and before it is used, rinse it twice in clear, cool water, using no soap, detergent, or bleach. Let the quilt air-dry.

For dark fabrics, the cleanest marker you can use is a thin sliver of pure, white **soap.** Choose a soap that contains no creams, deodorants, dyes, or perfumes; these added ingredients may leave a residue on the fabric.

Other marking tools include **colored pencils** made specifically for marking fabric and **tailor's chalk** (available in powdered, stick, and traditional cake form). When using chalk, mark small sections of the quilt at a time because the chalk rubs off easily.

Quilting Stencils

Quilting patterns can be purchased as precut stencils. Simply lay these on your quilt top and mark the design through the cutout areas.

To make your own stencil of a printed quilting pattern, such as the one below, use a permanent marker to trace the design onto a blank sheet of template plastic. Then use a craft knife to cut out the design.

Quilting Stencil Pattern

Making a Quilt Backing

Some fabric and quilt shops sell 90" and 108" widths of 100% cotton fabric that are very practical for quilt backing. However, the instructions in this book always give backing yardage based on 44"-wide fabric.

When using 44"-wide fabric, all quilts wider than 41" will require a pieced backing. For quilts 41" to 80" wide, you will need an amount of fabric equal to two times the desired *length* of the unfinished backing. (The unfinished backing should be at least 3" larger on all sides than the quilt top.)

The simplest method of making a backing is to cut the fabric in half widthwise **(Diagram 29)**, and then sew the two panels together lengthwise. This results in a backing with a vertical center seam. Press the seam allowances to one side.

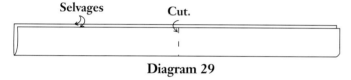

Diagram 29

Another method of seaming the backing results in two vertical seams and a center panel of fabric. This method is often preferred by quilt show judges. Begin by cutting the fabric in half widthwise. Open the two lengths and stack them, with right sides facing and selvages aligned. Stitch along *both* selvage edges to create a tube of fabric **(Diagram 30).** Cut down the center of the top layer of fabric only and open the fabric flat **(Diagram 31).** Press seam allowances to one side.

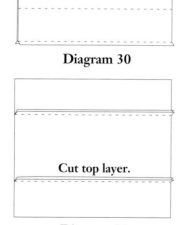

Diagram 30

Diagram 31

If the quilt is wider than 80", it is more economical to cut the fabric into three lengths that are the desired width of the backing. Join the three lengths so that the seams are horizontal to the quilt, rather than vertical. For this method, you'll need an amount of fabric equal to three times the *width* of the unfinished backing.

Fabric requirements in this book reflect the most economical method of seaming the backing fabric.

Layering and Basting

After the quilt top and backing are made, the next steps are layering and basting in preparation for quilting.

Prepare a large working surface to spread out the quilt—a large table, two tables pushed together, or the floor. Place the backing on the working surface wrong side up. Unfold the batting and place it on top of the backing, smoothing away any wrinkles or lumps.

Lay the quilt top wrong side down on top of the batting and backing. Make sure the edges of the backing and quilt top are parallel.

Knot a long strand of sewing thread and use a long (darning) needle for basting. Begin basting in the center of the quilt and baste out toward the edges. The basting stitches should cover an ample amount of the quilt so that the layers do not shift during quilting.

Machine quilters use nickel-plated safety pins for basting so there will be no basting threads to get caught on the presser foot. Safety pins, spaced approximately 4" apart, can be used by hand quilters, too.

Hand Quilting

Hand-quilted stitches should be evenly spaced, with the spaces between stitches about the same length as the stitches themselves. The *number* of stitches per inch is less important than the *uniformity* of the stitching. Don't worry if you take only five or six stitches per inch; just be consistent throughout the project.

Machine Quilting

For machine quilting, the backing and batting should be 3" larger all around than the quilt top, because the quilting process pushes the quilt top fabric outward. After quilting, trim the backing and batting to the same size as the quilt top.

Thread your bobbin with good-quality sewing thread (not quilting thread) in a color to match the backing. Use a top thread color to match the quilt top or use invisible nylon thread.

An even-feed or walking foot will feed all the quilt's layers through the machine at the same speed. It is possible to machine-quilt without this foot (by experimenting with tension and presser foot pressure), but it will be much easier *with* it. If you do not have this foot, get one from your sewing machine dealer.

Straight-Grain Binding

1. Mark the fabric in horizontal lines the width of the binding **(Diagram 32)**.

A	↕ width of binding	
B		A
C		B
D		C
E		D
F		E
		F

Diagram 32

2. With right sides facing, fold the fabric in half, offsetting drawn lines by matching letters and raw edges **(Diagram 33)**. Stitch a ¼" seam.

3. Cut the binding in a continuous strip, starting with one end and following the marked lines around the tube. Press the strip in half lengthwise.

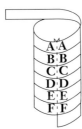

Diagram 33

Continuous Bias Binding

This technique can be used to make continuous bias for appliqué as well as for binding.

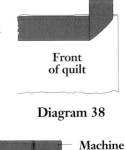

Diagram 34

1. Cut a square of fabric in half diagonally to form two triangles. With right sides facing, join the triangles **(Diagram 34)**. Press the seam allowance open.

2. Mark parallel lines the desired width of the binding **(Diagram 35)**, taking care not to stretch the bias. With right sides facing, align the raw edges (indicated as Seam 2). As you align the edges, offset one Seam 2 point past its natural matching point by one line. Stitch the seam; then press the seam allowance open.

Diagram 35

3. Cut the binding in a continuous strip, starting with the protruding point and following the marked lines around the tube **(Diagram 36)**. Press the strip in half lengthwise.

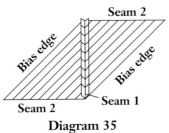

Diagram 36

Applying Binding

Binding is applied to the front of the quilt first. You may begin anywhere on the edge of the quilt except at the corner.

1. Matching raw edges, lay the binding on the quilt. Fold down the top corner of the binding at a 45° angle, align the raw edges, and pin **(Diagram 37)**.

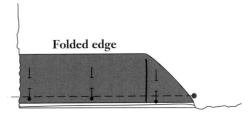

Folded edge

Diagram 37

2. Beginning at the folded end, machine-stitch the binding to the quilt. Stop stitching ¼" from the corner and backstitch. Fold the binding strip diagonally away from the quilt, making a 45° angle **(Diagram 38)**.

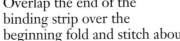

Front of quilt

Diagram 38

3. Fold the binding strip straight down along the next side to be stitched, creating a pleat in the corner. Position the needle at the ¼" seam line of the new side **(Diagram 39)**. Make a few stitches, backstitch, and then stitch the seam. Continue until all corners and sides are done. Overlap the end of the binding strip over the beginning fold and stitch about 2" beyond it. Trim any excess binding.

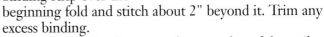

Machine stitching begins here.

Front of quilt

Diagram 39

4. Turn the binding over the raw edge of the quilt. Slipstitch it in place on the back, using thread that matches the binding. The fold at the beginning of the binding strip will create a neat, angled edge when it is folded to the back.

5. At each corner, fold the binding to form a miter **(Diagram 40)**. Hand-stitch the miters closed if desired.

Back of quilt

Diagram 40

Golden Double Wedding Ring

During a difficult period of her life, Linda Houghton found solace in creating this soft pastel quilt of stars and rings. When everything else seemed out of control, Linda found peace in the orderly assembly of her quilt, so she nicknamed it "Order Out of Chaos."

An avid quilter who learned the craft at her grandmother's knee, Linda devotes two to four hours a day to her quilting. She sewed all the center stars by hand, carrying the pieces around in a shoebox so that she could seize every opportunity to piece. She suggests that *Golden Double Wedding Ring* is a good quilt on which to practice piecing challenging curves and precise points, but she doesn't recommend that it be your first quilt. The set-in pieces and scalloped edges also require some expertise.

Quilt by Linda Houghton,
Rocky Hill, New Jersey

Finished Quilt Size

84" x 96½"

Fabric Requirements

Muslin	8½ yards*
Pink solid	3¼ yards
Pink print	1¼ yards
Blue solid	1¼ yards
Blue print	3¾ yards
Backing	8¼ yards

*Includes 1 yard for bias binding.

Number to Cut

Template A	300 pink solid
Template B	294 blue print
Template C	288 muslin
Template D	165 muslin
Template E	360 pink solid
Template F	330 pink print
Template F rev.	330 pink print
Template G	330 blue print
Template G rev.	330 blue solid
Template H	330 blue print
Template H rev.	330 blue solid
Template I	6 pink solid
Template I rev.	6 pink solid
Template J	6 blue print
Template J rev.	6 blue print
Template K	6 muslin
Template K rev.	6 muslin
Template L	6 pink print
Template L rev.	6 pink print
Template M	6 blue solid
	12 blue print
Template M rev.	6 blue solid
	12 blue print
Template N	6 blue solid
Template N rev.	6 blue solid
Template O	6 pink print
Template O rev.	6 pink print
Template P	30 muslin

Quilt Top Assembly

1. Join 6 As to form a star, as shown in **Diagram 1**. Make 46 stars.

2. Join Bs and Cs to each star, as shown in **Diagram 2**.

3. Referring to photograph for color placement and **Diagram 3**, assemble 1 E, 1 F, 1 G, 1 H, 1 H rev., 1 G rev., and 1 F rev. to make a pieced arc. Make 330 arcs with E at 1 end only, as shown in **Diagram 3**. Join arcs to Ds as shown to make ring segments.

4. Referring to **Diagram 4**, sew ring segments to stars, adding Es at ends as necessary to fit rings together.

5. Referring to **Diagram 5**, make 6 half-stars. Using L, Ms, N, and O, make arcs for each half-star. Join arcs to half-stars.

6. Starting from 1 side, join 4 vertical rows of stars; then join rows with remaining stars and half-stars. Referring to **Diagram 6**, use Ps to join ring segments on outside edges.

Quilting

Outline-quilt patchwork or quilt as desired.

Finished Edges

Referring to instructions on page 11, make 11 yards of 2"-wide continuous bias binding from 32" square of muslin. Apply binding to quilt edges, easing bias strip along curves and pivoting at corners along scalloped edge. Miter or tuck these corners. Fold binding to back and blindstitch in place.

Diagram 1   Diagram 2

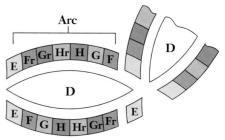

Diagram 3

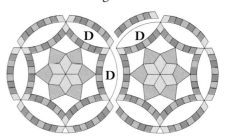

Diagram 4

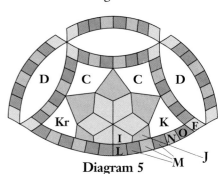

Diagram 5

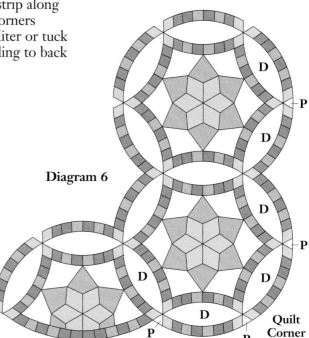

Diagram 6

B

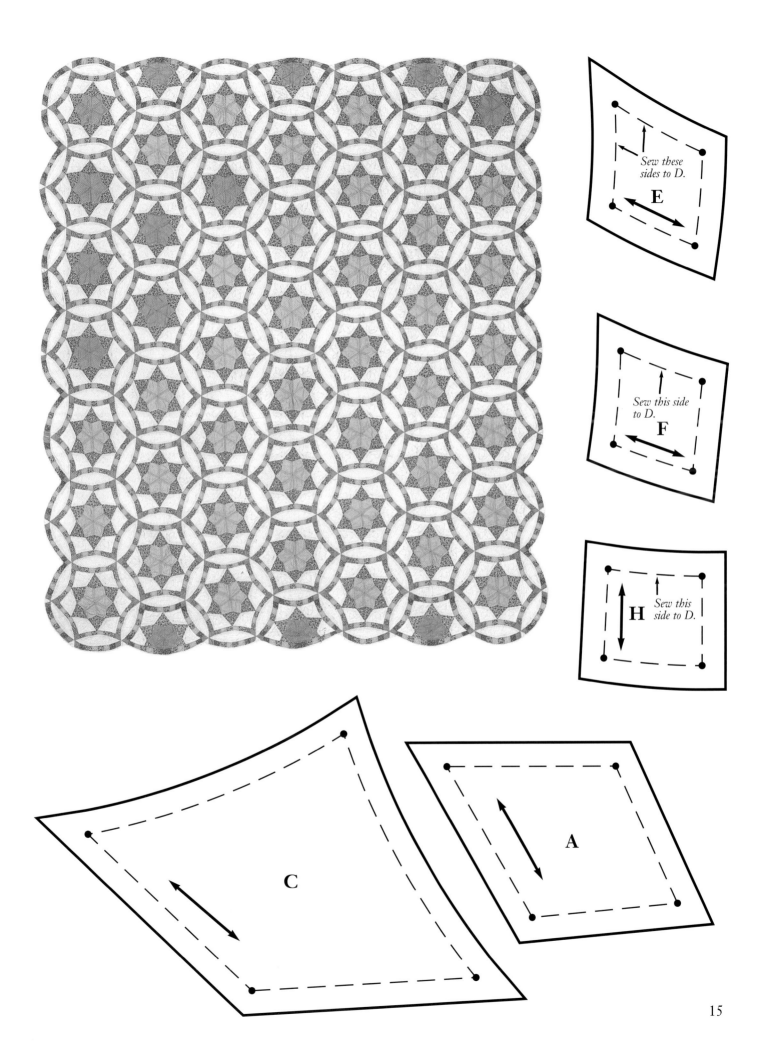

Sew these sides to D.

E

Sew this side to D.

F

H *Sew this side to D.*

C

A

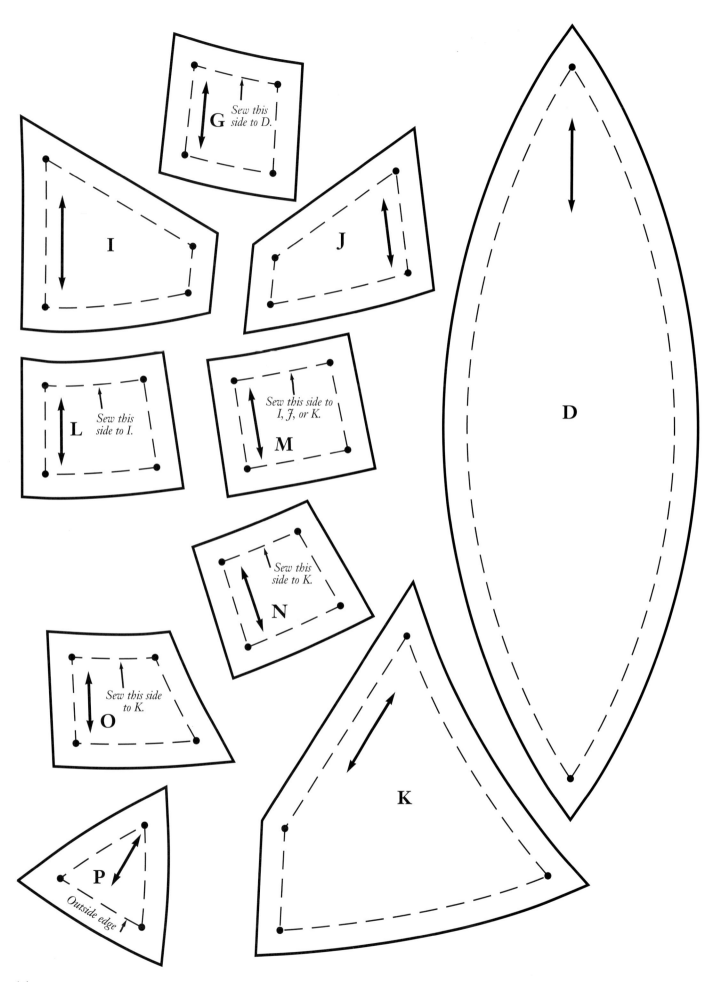

G Sew this side to D.

I

J

L Sew this side to I.

M Sew this side to I, J, or K.

D

N Sew this side to K.

O Sew this side to K.

P Outside edge

K

*Quilt by May Baker,
Scottsdale, Arizona*

Mexican Rose

May Baker made this quilt as a surprise for her daughter,
using the rich and mellow colors often seen in Mexican
crafts. The unity and completeness of the design are
enhanced by May's placement of small appliquéd squares
at the intersections of the blocks.

Finished Quilt Size
81" x 105"

Number of Blocks and Finished Size
48 blocks   12" x 12"

Fabric Requirements

Dark green	4 yards
White	3 yards
Light green	2¼ yards*
Rose stripe	2 yards
Backing	6⅛ yards

*Includes 32" square for binding.

Number to Cut**

Template A	255 dark green
	192 white
	48 light green
Template B	192 dark green
Template B rev.	192 dark green
Template C	192 rose stripe
Template D	384 light green
Template E	192 white

**See Step 1 to cut borders before cutting other pieces.

Quilt Top Assembly

1. From dark green, cut 2 (3½" x 101") strips and 2 (3½" x 83") strips for outer border. From white fabric, cut 2 (2" x 98") strips and 2 (2" x 77") strips for inner border. Set aside.

2. Referring to **Block Piecing Diagram,** join B, B rev., C, and Ds to make a corner unit. Make 4 corner units. Add 1 E to each side of 2 corner units. Join 9 As as shown to make center unit. Join units as shown. Make 48 blocks.

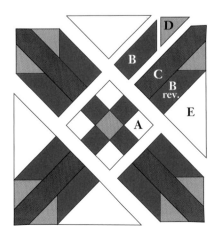

Block Piecing Diagram

3. Referring to photograph, join blocks in 8 rows of 6 blocks each. Join rows.

4. Sew longer white borders to quilt sides. Then sew remaining white borders to top and bottom edges. Join dark green outer borders in same manner.

5. Appliqué dark green A squares at intersections of blocks. Appliquéd squares will overlap white border on outside edge of block rows.

Quilting

Outline-quilt seams of blocks. Quilt borders as desired.

Finished Edges

Referring to instructions on page 11, make 10½ yards of 2½"-wide bias or straight-grain binding. Apply binding to quilt edges.

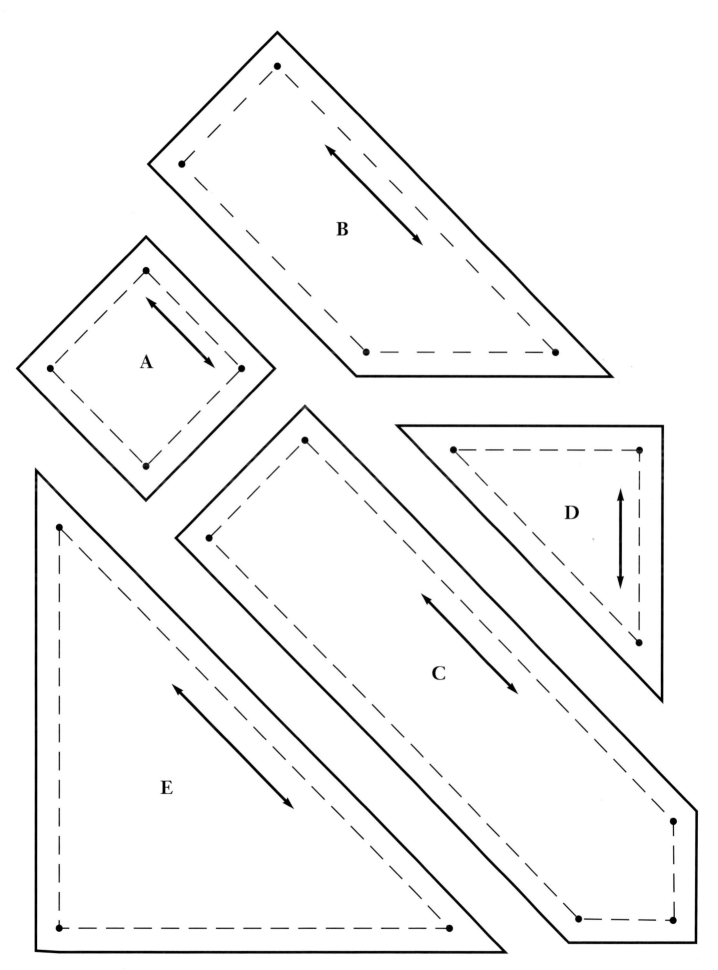

A

B

C

D

E

Feathered Friends

Fourteen of these Feathered Star blocks are the handi-work of Susan Danielson's quilting pals, who meet monthly to make and exchange blocks. Use fabrics of one color, as Susan did, or go for broke with random fabrics to create a freewheeling quilt of scrappy stars.

Unit Piecing Diagrams

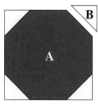

Unit A–Make 1.

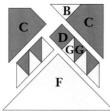

Unit F–Make 4.

Unit H–Make 4.

Block Assembly Diagram

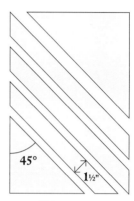

Diagram 1

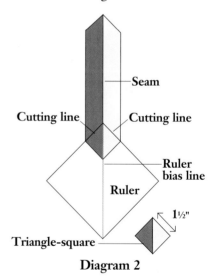

Diagram 2

Finished Quilt Size
89" x 103"

Number of Blocks and Finished Size
20 blocks   15" x 15"

Fabric Requirements
Muslin   10½ yards
20 medium
  blue prints   ½ yard each
20 dark blue
  prints   scraps
Binding fabric   1 yard
Backing   8¼ yards

Other Materials
6"-square acrylic ruler with bias line
Rotary cutter

Number to Cut*
Template A   20 dark blue
Template B   160 muslin
Template C   160 medium blue
Template D   160 medium blue
Template E   160 dark blue
Template F   80 muslin
Template G   960 muslin
         640 medium blue
4⅞" squares (H)   80 muslin
1½" squares (I)   4 muslin

*See steps 1 and 2 to cut borders, sashing,
  and pieces for triangle-squares before
  cutting other pieces.

Quilt Top Assembly
1. From muslin, cut borders and sashing as follows: 4 (4½" x 99") strips for outer border, 4 (1½" x 92") strips for middle border, 2 (6" x 82") strips and 2 (5" x 78") strips for inner border, 4 (1½" x 66") strips for horizontal sashing, and 15 (1½" x 15½") strips for vertical sashing. Set borders and sashing strips aside.

2. From muslin, cut 17 (14" x 18") pieces for triangle-squares. Cut 17 (14" x 18") pieces from assorted medium blue fabrics. Set rectangles aside.

3. To make 1 block, refer to **Unit Piecing Diagrams** to make 1 Unit A, 4 Unit Fs, and 4 Unit Hs. Following **Block Assembly Diagram,** join units in rows and join rows. Repeat to make 20 blocks.

4. Join 4 blocks with 3 (1½" x 15½") sashing strips to make 1 horizontal row. Repeat to make 5 rows.

5. Join rows with 66"-long sashing strips between rows.

6. Join 6"-wide inner border strips to quilt sides; then join 5"-wide strips to top and bottom edges.

7. For sawtooth border, pair each 14" x 18" muslin rectangle with 1 blue rectangle, with right sides facing and raw edges aligned. Referring to **Diagram 1,** use acrylic ruler to find a 45°-angle and rotary-cut 1½"-wide bias strips across each rectangle. Keeping strips paired, join each pair along longest edge, using a ¼" seam. Press seam allowances open.

8. Referring to **Diagram 2,** place square ruler on 1 pieced strip so that bias (45°) line aligns with seam. Rotary-cut 1 (1½") triangle-square as shown. Repeat to cut a total of 672 triangle-squares.

9. Referring to photograph for placement, join 90 triangle-squares to make 1 side border. Repeat to make second side border. Join borders to quilt sides.

10. Join 76 triangle-squares to make top border. Repeat to make bottom border. Join borders to top and bottom edges of quilt.

11. Sew 1 (92"-long) middle border to each quilt side. Trim remaining 92"-long borders to fit top and bottom edges; then join these to quilt.

12. Join 92 triangle-squares to make 1 side border. Repeat to make second side border. Join borders to quilt sides.

13. Join 78 triangle-squares to make top border, adding an I at each end. Repeat to make bottom border. Join borders to top and bottom edges of quilt.

14. Join 4½"-wide muslin borders to quilt in same manner as for previous borders, adding side borders first and then top and bottom borders.

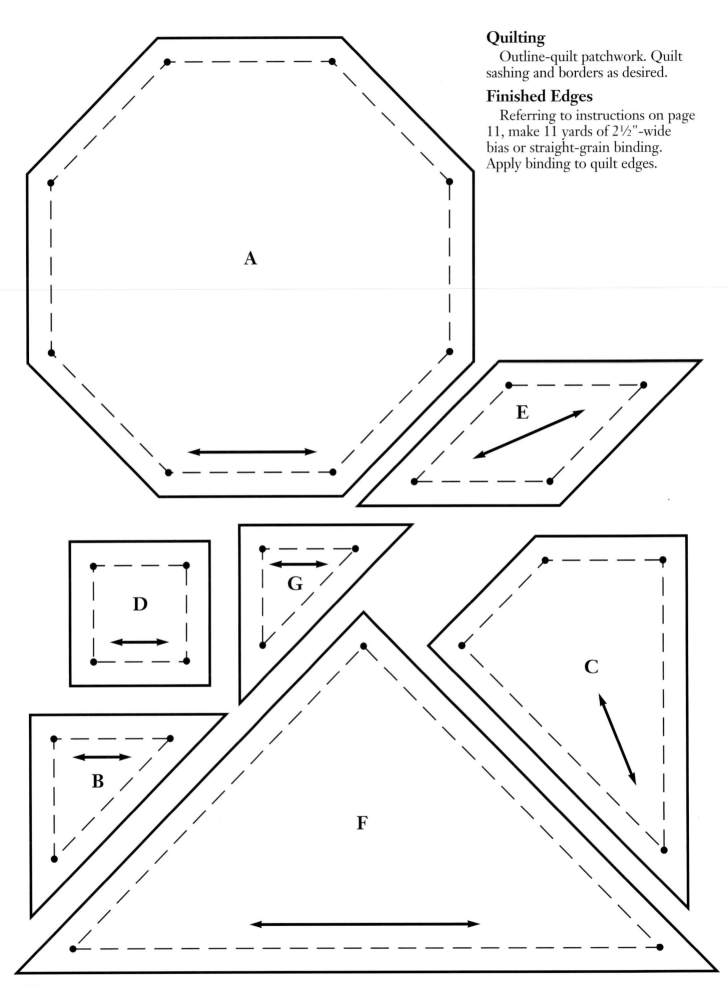

A

E

D

G

C

B

F

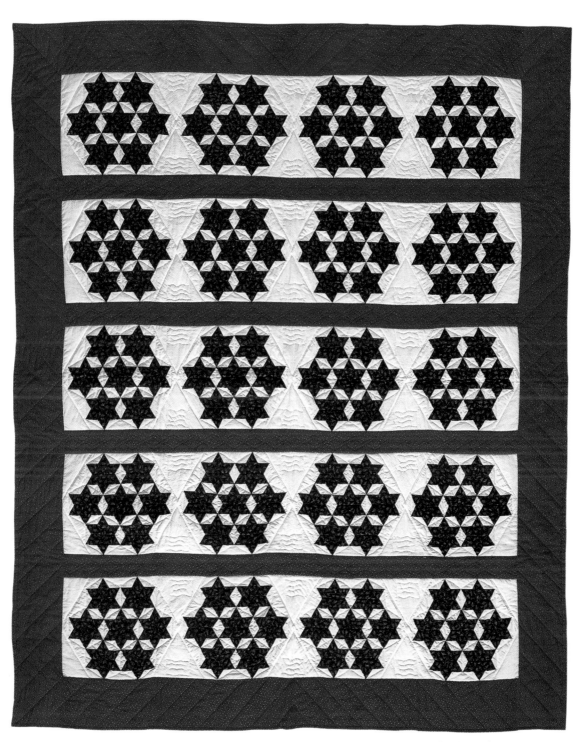

Quilt by Judy Cantwell,
Cahaba Heights, Alabama

Seven Sisters

A cluster of stars in the constellation Taurus is named for seven sisters of Greek myth who were turned into stars by the gods. These heavenly bodies inspired this traditional block of patchwork stars. Interpreted in patriotic red, white, and blue, this block is a hexagon instead of the usual square.

Finished Quilt Size

70" x 87⅝"

Number of Blocks and Finished Size

20 blocks   13⅛" x 15"

Fabric Requirements

Muslin	3½ yards
Blue print	3 yards
Red print	3 yards*
Backing	5⅜ yards

*Includes fabric for straight-grain binding.

Number to Cut

Template A	840 blue print
	360 muslin
Template B	120 muslin
Template C	30 muslin
Template D	10 muslin
Template D rev.	10 muslin

Quilt Top Assembly

1. Referring to **Star Diagram**, join 6 blue As to make a star. Make 7 stars for each block.

2. Referring to **Block Assembly Diagram,** join 7 stars with 18 muslin As and 6 Bs. (See page 6 for tips on sewing set-in seams.) In this manner, make 20 blocks.

3. Referring to **Row Assembly Diagram,** arrange blocks in 5 horizontal rows of 4 blocks each. Join blocks in each row with Cs as shown, ending each row with D and D rev. Press seam allowances toward Cs and Ds.

4. Cut 4 (3½"-wide) strips of red print for sashing. Join rows, alternating block rows and sashing strips.

5. Cut 4 (5½"-wide) strips of red print for borders. Add borders to quilt, mitering corners.

Quilting

Make stencils for flag and cable quilting designs. (See page 9 for tips on making stencils.) Mark flags in muslin triangles, positioning flags as shown on Pattern C. Mark cables in sashing strips.

Outline-quilt patchwork. Quilt flags and cables as marked and borders as desired.

Finished Edges

Referring to instructions on page 11, make 8¾ yards of 2½"-wide straight-grain binding from red print fabric. Apply binding to quilt edges.

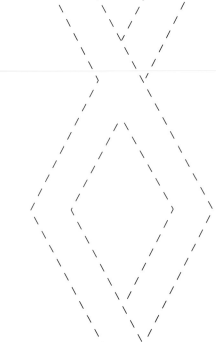

Cable Quilting Design

Star Diagram

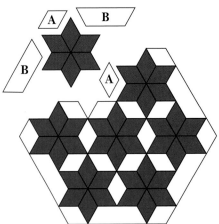

Block Assembly Diagram

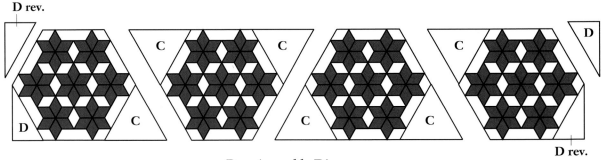

Row Assembly Diagram

24

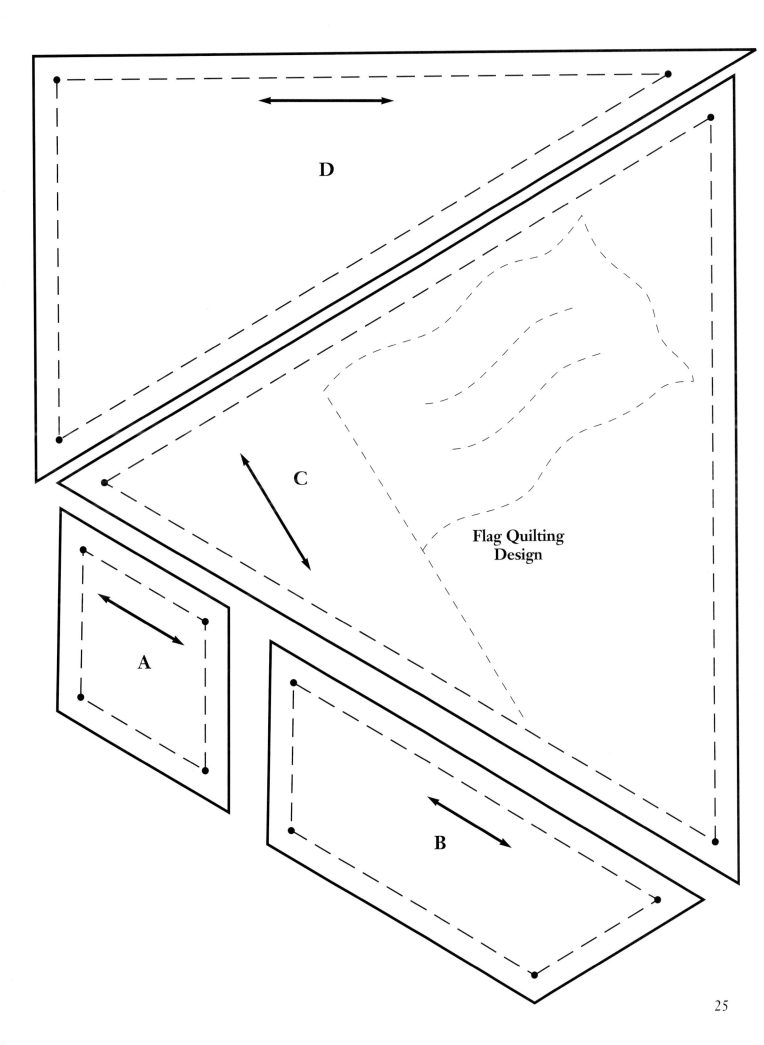

D

C

Flag Quilting
Design

A

B

Quilt by Elaine DeLancey Shinners,
Paradise, California

Folded Stars

An interest in folding techniques and a passion for quiltmaking led Elaine Shinners to create a quilt that combines the two. "I prefer to work with dimensional pieces and to design my own patterns," says Elaine, who teaches quilting in northern California. For this elegant but functional bridal quilt, Elaine mixed varied textures of crepe satin, lace, and eyelet.

These blocks should not be quilted, so Elaine used tying to anchor the folded pieces to the backing. Borders are attached after the blocks and sashing are tied.

Finished Quilt Size
82" x 96"

Number of Blocks and Finished Size
20 blocks   12" x 12"

Fabric Requirements

Muslin	6¾ yards
Peach eyelet	5 yards
Cream eyelet	4 yards
Ecru allover lace	3 yards
Peach satin	2 yards
Floral stripe	2⅛ yards
Backing	6 yards

Other Materials
2"-wide insertion
lace   19 yards
Fabric glue stick
Peach crochet thread (mercerized)
Large-eyed embroidery or tapestry
needle

Number to Cut*

5" squares (A)	100 peach satin	
	160 allover lace	
5¾" squares (B)	160 cream eyelet	
	80 peach eyelet	
7" squares (C)	80 peach eyelet	

*See steps 1 and 2 of block instructions to
cut borders and sashing before cutting
other pieces.

Folded Star Blocks

1. From floral stripe fabric, cut 4 (2¾" x 76") strips for inner border. From muslin, cut 4 (7" x 81") strips for outer borders. For sashing, cut the following from muslin: 5 (3" x 71") strips, 2 (3" x 62") strips, and 16 (3" x 12½") strips. Set borders and sashing aside.

2. Cut 20 (12½") squares of muslin for folded star backings. Lightly press each square in half horizontally, vertically, and diagonally to make 4 placement lines.

3. Center 1 peach satin A on each muslin square. Corners of A should align with diagonal placement lines. Anchor satin square with fabric glue.

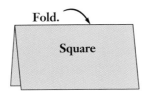
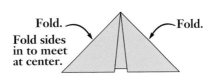

Folding Diagram 1

Folding Diagram 2

4. Referring to **Folding Diagram 1,** fold and press the following for *each* star: 4 peach satin As, 8 lace As, 8 cream eyelet Bs, and 4 peach eyelet Bs. Each folded piece is a *triangle.* Referring to **Folding Diagram 2,** fold and press 4 peach eyelet Cs to make folded *squares.*

5. Referring to **Placement Diagram,** place 1 peach satin triangle on each edge of anchored satin square for Layer 1 of folded star. Triangle points will meet at center. Tack points with matching thread. Baste raw edges in place through all layers.

6. For Layer 2, place 1 lace triangle *between* 2 satin triangles, with center of fold aligned with diagonal placement line and point ¾" from center of block. (See block photograph; each layer is numbered.) Position 4 triangles in this manner; then tack and baste in place.

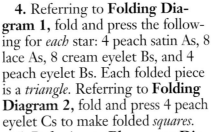

Placement Diagram

7. For Layer 3, position 4 lace triangles between Layer 2 triangles in same manner. Align, tack, and baste as before.

8. For layers 4 and 5, position cream eyelet triangles with points 1½" from center of block. Align, tack, and baste.

9. For Layer 6, position folded peach eyelet *squares* at corners (aligned with diagonal placement lines), placing point of square 2¼" from center of block. Tack and baste in place. For Layer 7, position peach eyelet triangles at each side with points 2¼" from center of block. Tack and baste as for previous layers.

10. Complete 20 Folded Star blocks.

11. From remaining floral stripe fabric, cut 40 (1⅝" x 10¼") strips and 40 (1⅝" x 12½") strips for block borders. Referring to block photograph, sew shorter strips to sides of each block through all layers; then sew longer strips to top and bottom edges.

Quilt Top Assembly

1. Cut pieces of insertion lace to match length of each muslin sashing strip. Center 1 lace strip on each sashing strip and topstitch.

2. Referring to **Setting Diagram,** alternate 5 star blocks with 4 sashing strips to make 1 vertical row. Make 4 vertical rows.

3. Join rows, adding 1 (71"-long) sashing strip between each row as shown. Sew 1 strip to each outer edge.

4. Join 62"-long sashing strips to top and bottom edges of assembled quilt top.

5. Cut 2 (39" x 63") pieces of backing fabric. Seam to make 1 (63" x 77") panel. Cut a matching batting piece. Layer backing, batting, and quilt top; pin-baste.

6. Cut 40 (8") lengths of crochet thread. Working from front of quilt, insert threaded needle in block center. Pull thread to back, leaving 1½" of thread on top of quilt. Bring needle from back to front and cut thread, leaving a 1½" length. Repeat with another thread piece. Tie threads loosely in a square knot at star center, as shown in block photograph. Trim threads to 1" long. Repeat for each block.

7. Cut backing and batting strips to match all strips for inner and outer borders.

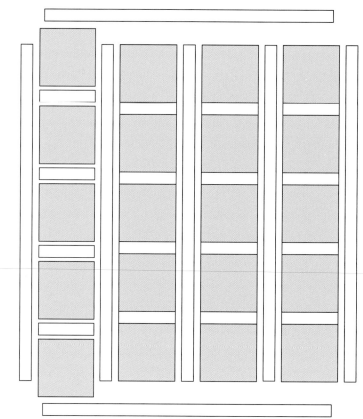

Setting Diagram

8. With right sides facing, match raw edge of 1 inner border strip with 1 side edge of quilt. Pin in place. With right sides facing, match raw edge of backing strip to same edge of quilt back and pin. Stitch through all layers. Repeat on opposite side of quilt.

9. Smooth border and backing strips flat, with wrong sides facing. Insert batting strip between layers and pin or baste to hold batting in place.

10. Join inner border strips to top and bottom edges in same manner. Then insert batting strips as before.

11. Join outer borders to quilt in same manner as for inner borders, joining side borders first and then top and bottom borders. Seams should catch inner border batting strips.

12. Machine-quilt down center of each border strip to anchor batting.

Finished Edges

1. Cut 136 (4") squares of muslin for prairie points. (If you have scraps of peach fabrics left, you might want to mix in some peach squares for accent.) Fold squares as described on page 43 to make prairie points.

2. Matching raw edges, pin prairie points to muslin borders, spacing them evenly around edge. Stitch prairie points in place, being careful not to catch backing.

3. Turn under raw edge of backing to cover raw edges of prairie points. Blindstitch backing hem in place.

Quilt by Pauline F. Spieks,
Stone Mountain, Georgia

Star and Crescent

Precision is the key to success here. Refer to the Workshop for tips on careful cutting, piecing curved seams, and pressing seam allowances. A stunning quilt will be the reward for your extra care.

Finished Quilt Size
102" x 117"

Number of Blocks and Finished Size
42 blocks   15" x 15"

Fabric Requirements
Muslin	10 yards
Red print	7 yards*
Backing	9 yards

*Includes 1 yard for binding.

Number to Cut**
Template A	168	red print
Template B	168	muslin
Template C	168	red print
Template D	168	muslin
Template E	78	red print
Template F	4	red print
Template G	82	red print

**See Step 1 to cut borders before cutting other pieces.

Quilt Top Assembly

1. From muslin, cut 4 (6½" x 121") strips for borders. Set aside.

2. Referring to **Block Assembly Diagram,** join 1 B to 1 C to make a pieced cone. Repeat to make 168 cones.

3. For each block, join 4 cones and 4 As to make a star; then add Ds at corners to complete block as shown. Make 42 blocks.

4. Referring to photograph, arrange blocks in 7 horizontal rows of 6 blocks each. Join blocks in rows. Join rows to assemble quilt top.

5. Mark centers on edges of each border strip. Mark centers on edges of quilt. Matching centers of borders and quilt edges, join border strips to all edges. See page 8 for instructions on mitering border corners.

6. Turn under edges on Es, Fs, and Gs. Referring to photograph, center 1 F over each mitered seam and pin. Pin 18 Es on top and bottom borders and 21 Es on each side border as shown. Pin Gs over ends where scallops meet. Appliqué all pieces.

Quilting
Outline-quilt patchwork and appliqué. Add other quilting as desired.

Finished Edges
Referring to instructions on page 11, make 12¼ yards of 2½"-wide bias or straight-grain binding from red print fabric. Apply binding to quilt edges.

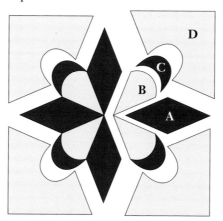

Block Assembly Diagram

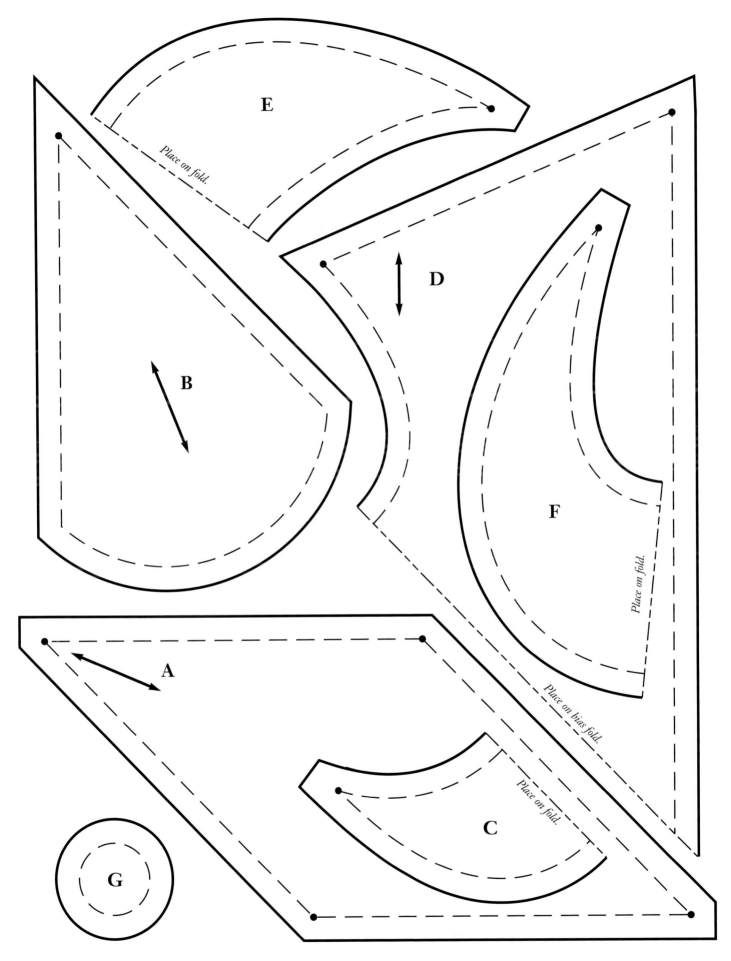

E

Place on fold.

B

D

F

Place on fold.

A

Place on bias fold.

C

Place on fold.

G

31

Quilt by Judy Cantwell,
Cahaba Heights, Alabama

In the Bleak Midwinter

As a haunting melody transforms Christina Rossetti's poem of winter chill into a favorite hymn, so can seemingly drab fabrics mix to prove that even the easiest piecing can bring dramatic results. For years, Judy Cantwell collected black prints with the idea of making this quilt someday. When that day came, she was ready with a pile of assorted scraps.

Finished Quilt Size
76½" x 88"

Number of Blocks and Finished Size
30 blocks   11½" x 11½"

Fabric Requirements
Light gray   4 yards
Black print
    for border   2¼ yards
Assorted black
    prints   scraps*
Black solid
    for binding   1 yard
Backing   5¼ yards

*Use scraps or select ¼ yard each of 11 fabrics.

Number to Cut**
Template A†   480 light gray
              480 assorted black prints

**See Step 1 to cut borders before cutting other pieces.

†See Alternate Quick Piecing instructions before cutting.

Quilt Top Assembly
1. From light gray fabric, cut 4 (3½" x 72") strips for inner borders. Set aside.

2. Referring to **Piecing Diagram,** join 1 black triangle and 1 gray triangle to make a triangle-square. Make 480 triangle-squares.

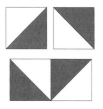

Piecing Diagram

3. Join triangle-squares in pairs; then combine pairs to make a 4-square unit, as shown in **Piecing Diagram.**

4. Referring to **Block Assembly Diagram** for color placement, join 4 pieced units to make 1 block. Repeat to make 30 blocks.

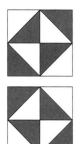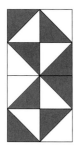

Block Assembly Diagram

Alternate Quick Piecing
Triangle-squares can be pre-assembled to save time. Quick piecing eliminates the labor of making a template, tracing it repeatedly on fabric, cutting out each piece, and joining one pair at a time. This technique involves marking a grid on the wrong side of 1 fabric piece and stitching diagonal lines through the grid.

1. Instead of using Template A, cut 24 (9" x 21") pieces from gray fabric. Cut matching pieces from assorted black prints.

2. On wrong side of each gray piece, mark a 2- x 5-square grid of 3¾" squares, as shown in **Diagram 1.** Draw diagonal lines through squares as shown.

3. With right sides facing, pin a gray rectangle to each black piece.

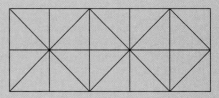

Diagram 1

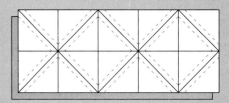

Diagram 2

4. Machine-stitch ¼" from each side of all *diagonal* lines, as shown in **Diagram 2.**

5. Cut on *all* grid lines to separate triangle-squares.

5. Referring to photograph, arrange blocks in 6 horizontal rows of 5 blocks each. Join blocks in rows. Join rows to assemble quilt top.

6. Mark centers on edges of each gray border strip. Mark centers on edges of quilt. Matching centers of borders and quilt, join border strips to all edges. See page 8 for instructions on mitering border corners.

7. For outer borders, cut 4 (7"-wide) strips of black print fabric. Add mitered borders to quilt as before.

Quilting
Quilt each block as shown in **Quilting Diagram.** Extend lines of quilting from blocks into borders.

Finished Edges
Referring to instructions on page 11, make 9¼ yards of 2½"-wide bias or straight-grain binding. Apply binding to quilt edges.

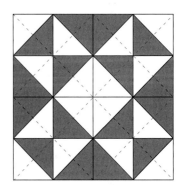

Quilting Diagram

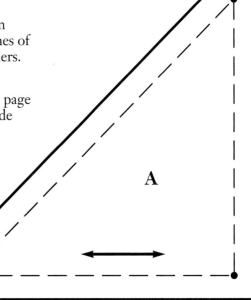

A

Quilt by Arleen Boyd,
Rochester, New York

Stars Over My Garden Maze

Like constellations ablaze in the inky dark of winter
skies, pieced stars shine brightly in this classic Garden
Maze setting. All the kaleidoscopic star centers can be
cut from one fabric with the use of a window template.

Finished Quilt Size
74" x 93½"

Number of Blocks and Finished Size
12 blocks   12" x 12"

Fabric Requirements
Floral print	3 yards
Navy	3 yards*
Tan	2¾ yards
Stripe	1 yard
24 assorted prints	scraps
Red miniprint	¼ yard
Backing	5¾ yards

*Includes ⅞ yard for binding.

Number to Cut**
Template A	96	floral†
Template B	96	assorted prints
Template C	96	assorted prints
Template D	96	stripe
Template F	40	navy
Template G	80	floral
Template H	20	navy

**See steps 1 and 2 to cut borders and star centers before cutting other pieces.

†Cut 8 per star from 1 fabric.

Quilt Top Assembly
1. Cut 8 (5" x 50") strips from floral print and 16 (2" x 50") strips from navy for strip-pieced sashing. Cut 2 (4" x 98") strips and 2 (4" x 80") strips from tan for border. Set aside.

2. Arleen used 1 floral print for all As, but each star center looks different. She positioned a window template over the same flowers in precisely the same manner to cut 8 As for 1 star, selecting a different portion of the fabric pattern for each star. (See page 4 for tips on making and using a window template.) Yardage allows extra for experimentation and selective template placement.

3. Referring to **Block Assembly Diagram,** join 8 As and 8 Bs to make 8 diamonds. Press seam allowances toward As in 4 diamonds and toward Bs in 4 diamonds. Selecting diamonds with opposing seam allowances, join diamonds in pairs as shown.

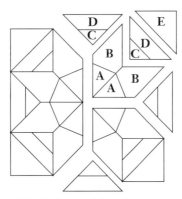

Block Assembly Diagram

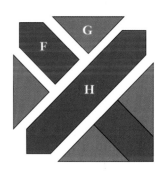

Sashing Square Assembly Diagram

4. Join 8 Cs and 8 Ds as shown. Press seam allowances toward Ds. Add Es to 4 C/D units. Set 1 C/D/E unit into opening in each diamond pair.

5. Join 2 diamond pairs as shown to make half of star; then set 1 C/D triangle into new opening. Repeat with remaining diamonds.

6. Join star halves. Set remaining C/D triangles into openings.

7. Repeat steps 3–6 to make 12 blocks.

8. Referring to **Sashing Square Assembly Diagram,** join Gs to sides of each F. Press seam allowance toward Fs. Join G/F/G triangles to sides of each H to make 20 sashing squares.

9. For sashing strips, join 1 (2" x 50") navy strip to sides of each 5" x 50" floral strip. Referring to **Sashing Strip Assembly Diagram,** cut 4 (12½"-long) segments from each strip set.

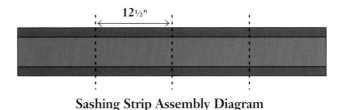

12½"

Sashing Strip Assembly Diagram

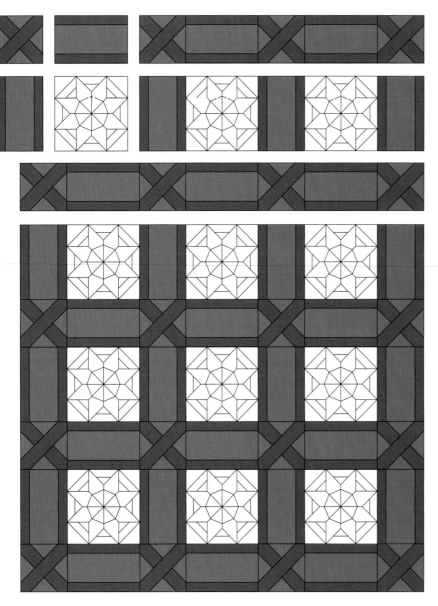

10. Referring to **Setting Diagram,** arrange blocks in 4 horizontal rows of 3 blocks each with sashing strips between blocks. Join blocks and sashing strips in each row. Add sashing strips to ends of rows. Press seam allowances toward sashing.

11. To make each horizontal sashing row, join 4 sashing squares and 3 sashing strips as shown. Make 5 sashing rows.

12. Join sashing rows and block rows.

13. Cut 10 (¾" x 42") strips from red for inner border. Join 3 strips end-to-end for each side border. Join 2 strips for top and bottom borders.

14. Mark centers of edges of each red and tan border strip. Matching centers, join red and tan strips in pairs. Trim red borders to match length of tan borders.

15. Mark centers on edges of quilt. Matching centers of borders and quilt, join border strips to all edges. See page 8 for instructions on mitering border corners.

Quilting

Outline-quilt patchwork. Quilt straight lines in tan border, perpendicular to seams and spaced 1" apart. Add other quilting as desired.

Finished Edges

Referring to instructions on page 11, make 9½ yards of 2½"-wide bias or straight-grain binding from navy fabric. Apply binding to quilt edges.

Setting Diagram

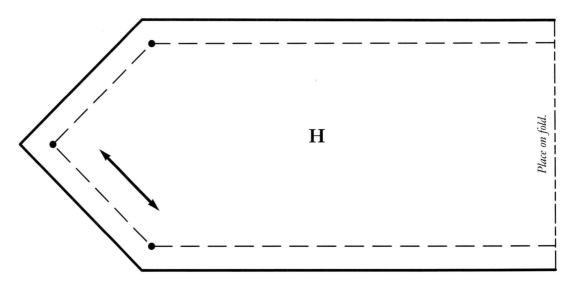

H

Place on fold.

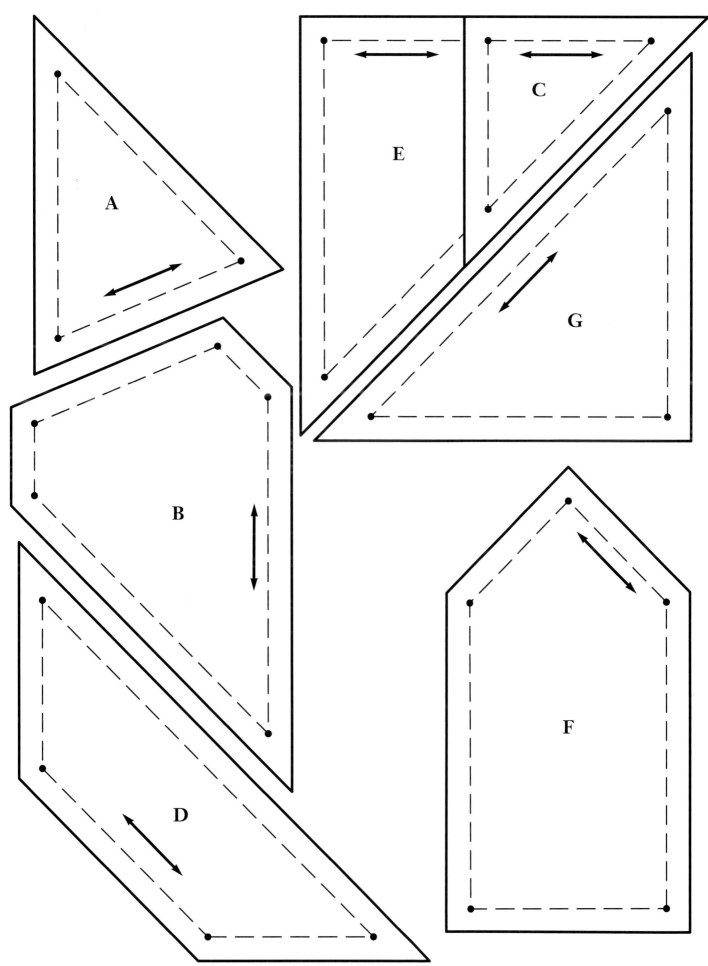

Quilt by Pauline Warren,
Sidney, Ohio

Delectable Mountain Star

This scrap quilt of geometric shapes is ideal for rotary cutting. Pauline Warren's imaginative setting creates a patchwork frame around a radiating medallion star. Using 16 scrap fabrics, she mixed and matched two fabrics to make each block.

Finished Quilt Size

77¾" x 77¾"

Number of Blocks and Finished Size

108 blocks   6⅞" x 6⅞"

Fabric Requirements

16 dark prints	Fat quarter each
Tan	4½ yards
Binding fabric	1 yard
Backing	4¾ yards

Number to Cut*

5" squares (A)	5 of each print
2¼" squares (B)	36 of each print
	420 tan
1⅞" squares (C)	140 tan
7¾" squares (D)	54 tan
7⅜" squares (E)	4 tan

*See Step 1 before cutting pieces.

Quilt Top Assembly

1. To get A, B, and D triangles, cut each appropriate square in half diagonally. These cutting instructions give you a few more As and Bs than you need, which will enable you to experiment with color combinations before piecing mountains.

2. Referring to **Mountain Assembly Diagram,** pick fabrics for each mountain, choosing 1 A of 1 print and 8 Bs of another print. Select fabric combinations for 140 mountains.

3. For each mountain, join 6 print Bs to 6 tan Bs to make 6 triangle-squares. Referring to **Mountain Assembly Diagram** for positioning of fabrics, join triangle-squares in 2 rows of 3. Join 1 print B to tan end of each strip. Join 1

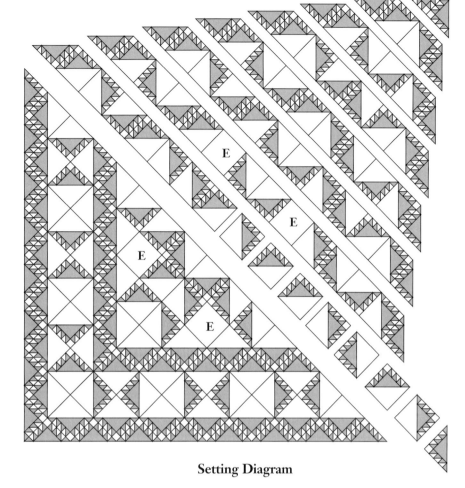

Setting Diagram

strip to 1 side of A as shown. Press seam allowances toward A. Join 1 C to remaining strip; then join strip to A to complete mountain. Make 140 mountains.

4. Referring to **Block Assembly Diagram,** join 1 D to 1 mountain to make a block. Make 108 blocks. (Remaining 32 mountains will be used for quilt borders.)

5. Referring to **Setting Diagram,** arrange mountains, blocks, and Es in diagonal rows. When satisfied with color placement, join pieces in rows.

6. Join rows to complete quilt top.

Quilting

Outline-quilt patchwork. Add other quilting as desired.

Finished Edges

Referring to instructions on page 11, make 9 yards of 2½"-wide bias or straight-grain binding. Apply binding to quilt edges.

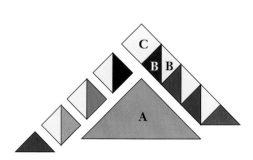

Mountain Assembly Diagram

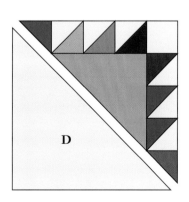

Block Assembly Diagram

Quilt by Rita Hays,
Grand Island, Nebraska

International Ohio Star

Quilters from the United States, Australia, and
England contributed blocks for this quilt, one of several
made in an international friendship project. Rita Hays
made the quilt using partial seaming techniques to avoid
seams in the middle of the sashing stars.

Finished Quilt Size
70" x 86"

Number of Blocks and Finished Size
12 blocks   12" x 12"

Fabric Requirements
Muslin	2 yards
Light blue	2½ yards
Navy print	3¼ yards
Assorted prints	scraps
Backing	5 yards

Number to Cut*
4½" squares (A)	56	muslin
	4	navy print
	4	assorted prints
Template B	48	muslin
	160	light blue
	18	navy print
	144	assorted prints
Template C	31	navy print
6⅛" squares (D)	20	muslin

*See Step 1 to cut borders and sashing before cutting other pieces.

Quilt Top Assembly

1. From light blue, cut 2 (1½" x 80") strips and 2 (1½" x 64") strips for inner border. From navy print, cut 2 (4½" x 73") strips and 2 (4½" x 89") strips for outer border and 14 (4½" x 12½") strips for side sashing. Set borders and sashing aside.

2. For each block, select 8 Bs of 1 print and 4 Bs of another print.

Referring to **Block Assembly Diagram,** join 4 Bs to make a square. Make 4 B squares as shown. Join B squares with muslin As in 3 rows as shown. Join rows to complete block. Make 8 blocks in this manner. Make 4 more blocks with print As in center.

3. To make vertical sashing, join 4 light blue Bs to 1 C, as shown in **Vertical Sashing Unit Diagram,** leaving seams incomplete on 2 triangles. (Partial seams are needed when Ds are inserted later.) Make 16 vertical sashing units. In same manner, make 15 horizontal sashing units, as shown in **Horizontal Sashing Unit Diagram.**

4. Arrange blocks in 4 rows of 3 blocks each. Referring to photograph, position blocks with print centers in first and fourth rows. Sew 1 horizontal sashing unit to top edge of each block.

5. Referring to **Row Assembly Diagram,** join blocks in each row, alternating blocks with 4 vertical sashing units.

6. To make triangle units for side sashing, join each navy print B to 1 light blue B. Referring to **Triangle Unit Diagram,** sew another light blue B to each pair, leaving seam incomplete as shown. Make 18 triangle units for side sashing.

7. Sew 1 triangle unit to 1 end of each side sashing strip. Referring to **Row Assembly Diagram,** join 1 side sashing unit to ends of each row to complete rows.

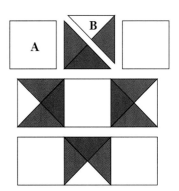

Block Assembly Diagram

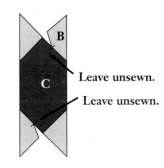

Vertical Sashing Unit Diagram

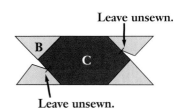

Horizontal Sashing Unit Diagram

Triangle Unit Diagram

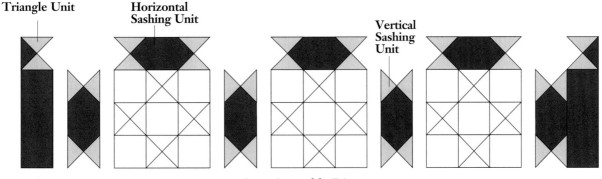

Row Assembly Diagram

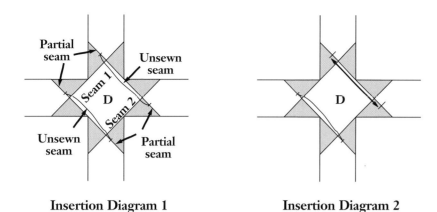

Insertion Diagram 1

Insertion Diagram 2

8. Arrange rows as shown in **Setting Diagram.** To complete fourth row, add horizontal sashing units and triangle units to bottom of row.

9. Join remaining sashing units, triangle units, and navy print As to make top and bottom sashing rows, as shown in **Setting Diagram.**

10. Join rows, leaving open areas for insertion of Ds.

11. Sew Ds to opposite sides of sashing units, as indicated by Seam 1 and Seam 2 in **Insertion Diagram 1.** Then stitch remaining 2 sides, closing each seam where partial seams ended, as indicated by arrow in **Insertion Diagram 2.**

12. Mark centers on edges of each light blue border strip. Mark centers on edges of quilt. Matching centers of borders and quilt, join borders to quilt. See page 8 for instructions on mitering border corners. Then join navy print borders to quilt in same manner.

Quilting

Outline-quilt patchwork. Add other quilting as desired.

Finished Edges

Cut 212 (3") squares from assorted prints for prairie points. See tip box on page 43 to make prairie points and finish edges.

Setting Diagram

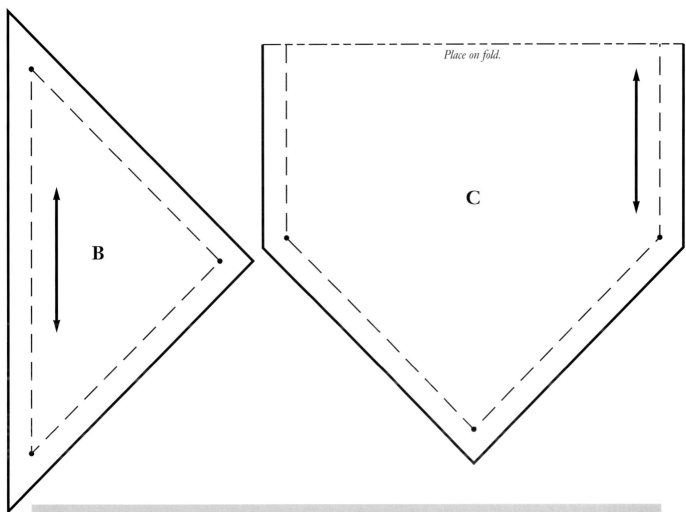

B

C

Place on fold.

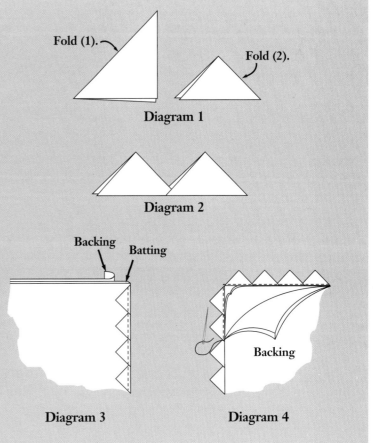

Making Prairie Points

Prairie points—fabric squares that are folded to make triangles—are often used to add interest to the edge of a quilt. The size of the square needed for folding is specified in instructions for each quilt. Follow these instructions to fold and stitch prairie points.

1. Referring to **Diagram 1,** fold each square in half diagonally. Fold again as shown to make a smaller triangle. Press triangles.

2. Referring to **Diagram 2,** arrange triangles in a continuous, overlapping line on quilt top, matching raw edges of quilt and prairie points. Baste.

3. Referring to **Diagram 3,** sew prairie points to quilt top only, keeping batting and backing out of the way.

4. Referring to **Diagram 4,** turn under edges of backing. Blindstitch backing over prairie point seam allowances.

Fold (1).

Fold (2).

Diagram 1

Diagram 2

Backing

Batting

Backing

Diagram 3

Diagram 4

Quilt by Charlotte Cameron,
Glenshaw, Pennsylvania

Summer Stars

Charlotte Cameron used 185 fabrics to hand-piece
this sunny cascade of pastel stars. Because there are no
separate borders, you can easily make the quilt smaller
or larger by changing the number of stars in each row.

Finished Quilt Size

Approximately 100" x 110"

Fabric Requirements

400 scraps	4" x 8" each
White	4 yards
Backing	9 yards

Number to Cut

Template A	480 blue
	480 pink
	480 green
	480 orange
	480 yellow
	1,121 white

Quilt Top Assembly

1. Referring to **Star Diagram,** join 6 As of 1 fabric to make a star. Make 400 stars.

2. Select 20 stars of 1 color group. Join stars in a row, adding white As between stars, as shown in **Row Assembly Diagram.** Make 20 rows.

3. Referring to photograph, arrange rows as desired. Join rows with white As, as shown in **Setting Diagram.**

Quilting

Outline-quilt patchwork or quilt as desired.

Finished Edges

Trim backing even with jagged edges of quilt top. Trim batting slightly smaller. Turn under edges of quilt top and backing; blind-stitch backing to quilt top.

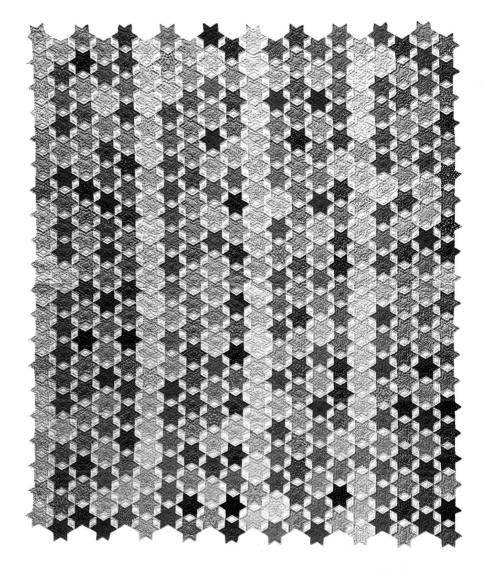

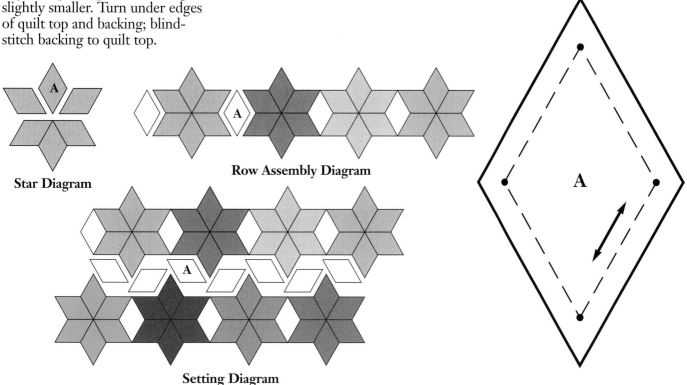

Star Diagram

Row Assembly Diagram

Setting Diagram

Quilt by Arthur A. Bluj,
Winston-Salem, North Carolina

Storm at Sea

Pieced sashing in this dramatic quilt creates the illusion
of stars on a storm-tossed sea. An all-time favorite, this
block is traditionally interpreted in nautical blue and white
fabrics. Different color schemes, even a scrap-bag approach,
are guaranteed to please in this sure-fire classic.

Finished Quilt Size
76" x 88"

Number of Blocks and Finished Size
42 large blocks 8" x 8"
56 small blocks 4" x 4"
97 sashing blocks 4" x 8"

Fabric Requirements
White   5¼ yards
Blue   2¾ yards
Navy   3 yards
Binding fabric   1 yard
Backing   5¼ yards

Number to Cut
Template A   42 blue
Template B   168 white
Template C   168 blue
Template D   97 navy
Template E   388 white
Template F   56 blue
Template G   224 white
Template H   224 navy

Quilt Top Assembly
1. Referring to **Block Assembly Diagram,** join 4 Bs to each A. Press seam allowances toward Bs. Join 4 Cs as shown to complete block. Press seam allowances toward Cs. Make 42 large blocks.

2. In same manner, join Fs, Gs, and Hs to make 56 small blocks.

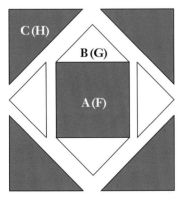

(Letters in parentheses indicate templates for small blocks.)

Block Assembly Diagram

3. Referring to **Sashing Block Assembly Diagram,** join 4 Es to each D. Press seam allowances toward Ds. Make 97 sashing blocks.

Sashing Block Assembly Diagram

4. Referring to photograph, arrange 7 small blocks in a row, alternating with 6 sashing blocks. Join blocks to make 1 sashing row. Repeat to make 8 sashing rows.

5. Referring to photograph, arrange 6 large blocks in a row, alternating with 7 sashing blocks. Join blocks to make 1 block row. Make 7 block rows.

6. Beginning with a sashing row, arrange rows, alternating sashing rows and block rows, as shown in photograph. Join rows to complete quilt top.

Quilting
Outline-quilt patchwork. Add other quilting as desired.

Finished Edges
Referring to instructions on page 11, make 9¼ yards of 2½"-wide bias or straight-grain binding. Apply binding to quilt edges.

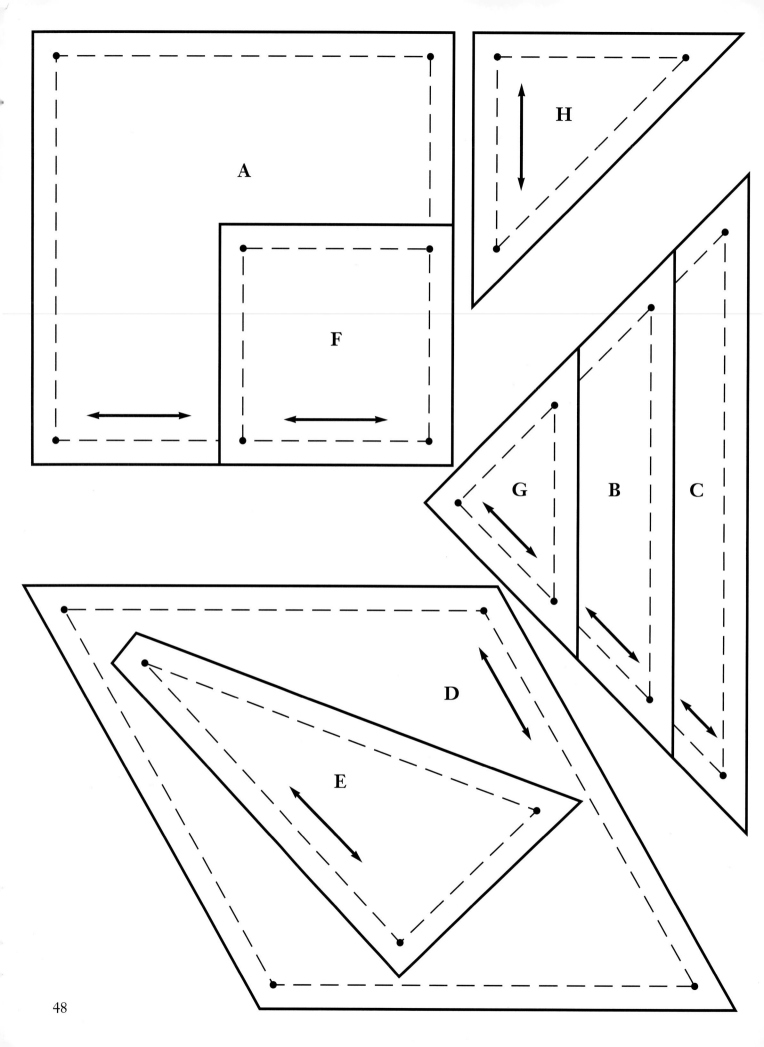